BREATHING IN SPRING

NADIA RASHA KHANSA

To Juwan, this is my love letter to you,

and to myself

To my grandmother, Rosa, you live on in every flower in this world.

CONTENTS

Introduction

Content Warning: This poetry collection contains references to sexual violence, suicide, mental illness, and war. Please be advised if those are potential triggers for you as you read this book. The content is most present in the first 2 chapters.

Despite the ominous content warning, this is not just a book about gratuitous pain. This is a book about my experiences with pain, and, more importantly, my constant, ever changing journey towards healing. One reason I felt compelled to write and share this collection of poems is because I know how deeply I have been helped by the words of other survivors.

As a survivor of sexual violence, a multi-ethnic American, and someone who has struggled with mental health my entire life, I've often been witness to the stories people assume about me and narratives that have been thrust on me without my consent. I have felt the heat of stigma in so many different aspects of my life that there have been times where I felt quite small and crushed beneath that weight. But the thing is, I am not ashamed of a single thing I mention in this book. I am not embarrassed by anything that has happened to me, and I've also come to a point where these memories are not the painful triggers they used to be.

The biggest reason I wanted to put all of this to words, is so that this collection serves as an act of reclaiming my life from everyone who has ever felt they could take it from me. I get to decide what meaning my story has in my life, and the act of speaking very openly about things that have been shushed into dark corners has felt extremely liberating and powerful.

I hope that in reading my book you can see yourself in the different spaces of darkness, and feel what it means to become free of past shackles.

DYING

How sad to die so young

Two Worlds Collided

In a small city of fewer than 300,000 people

Two immigrants gave a nod at the American Dream

A Guatemalan woman

Met a Lebanese man

He didn't speak Spanish

She didn't speak Arabic

And they fell in love with their second language

Beginning

Lebanon is the most beautiful country in the world. I have known this since I was the wise age of 5, and I knew everything (don't question it.) As far as I was concerned, I didn't need to see any of the other countries to make an empirically sound comparison--I just knew. Lebanon had everything a person could possibly want in such a small area--you could go skiing and to the beach on the same day, and it would only be a 2-hour drive or so. As a child, I remember creeping into thousand-year-old caves, fearfully clutching my father's hand with an iron grip, and jumping into ice-cold rivers with my siblings (and totally regretting it as soon as the cold shock struck). I got to gawk at the vast Roman ruins decorating the city of Baalbak, and have adults joke with me on hikes that I "don't eat the grass"--because we were hiking in fields of weed and possibly opioids. To this day, when I am sad, or happy, or stressed, or in any particularly extreme mood, I find myself yearning for the familiarity of Lebanese food. It's famously delicious, but in my heart, it's so much more than that: it's the ultimate comfort food that hits the spot just right every time. It tastes like home, it tastes like my childhood, and it tastes delicious. And yet, perhaps the most interesting thing about Lebanon is that, according to the History Channel, the previously mentioned Roman ruins are theorized to be an alien-landing site--and I totally believe it. When I was seven years old I definitely saw a blue girl with eight eyes peeking at me from the top of one of the historic pillars (they were very tall.) She had my haircut and crawled like she was on *The Exorcist* –remember, aliens are in Baalbek, Lebanon, and you heard it here first.

Home

Nothing compares

To the sense of comfort that goes unnoticed by most people

Hearing the mosque sing *adhan* five times a day

And the sound of Arabic being spoken by everyone around

Feeling safe with the familiar sounds

Seeing a car appear on the horizon

And wondering which of my 14 aunts and uncles it was

With how many of my fifty-something cousins?

Wondering

What memories would we make today?

Or in Ramadan, being woken at 3 a.m. each day

By a guy marching the streets with a drum

So we all knew, it was breakfast time

Never aware of the lights in our neighbors' windows

Telling us they were up too

And smelling the freshly baked pita bread and manoushe

Exuding from the cracked windows of the bakery

Who had also woken up early, to make sure we could eat before sunrise

All of those things indicating

We were where we were meant to be

And we were not alone

How can people who've seen such tragedy

still find the energy

To let the mountains echo with the sounds of unabashed laughter

Zaghareets and *durbake*s

And the unforgettable joy of *3amtous* reciting poetry?

Our strength is in our kindness

To a child's eye our people seemed bullet proof

No amount of horror in our history could dare to stifle the warmth

of our hearts as hot as fire

Why else would so many people seek to live in this paradise?

Our home became an embassy of strangers

a sanctuary for foreigners who would hear

of this Lebanese family who spoke English and Spanish

So whether you were the Swiss-Chilean-Lebanese billionaires across
the street

Who had lions and bears for pets

Or the humble traveling nature preservationists from Colorado

Or the German backpackers looking for someone to play soccer with

Or the French family whose kids answered the door in their birthday
suits

～

Or The-British-family-whose-kids-we-didn't-like-but-our-moms-were-friends-so-we-had-to-be-friends

Or The-British-family-who-we-*loved*-and-had-tons-of-sleepovers-with

You will be treated with all the warmth reserved for the most special guests

You will feel like family because you are family

and then you will realize

you are home too.

Magic Little Secrets

I had a routine on weekends

I'd wake up before sunrise

Sneak into our backyard

Ransack our blackberry tree and feast on my loot

--but leaving two or three survivors

So when my dad woke up he'd see it was fruitful

and never be aware that most goods were stolen

Then, instead of walking out of the front gate

I'd scale the walls guarding our backyard

And walk into the tiny bit of forest by our house

Find somewhere to sit

And wait for something magical to happen.

Then I'd sneak back in

And pretend I spent my morning watching TV

My magic little secrets tucked behind my smile

Rose Gardens in Lebanon

Once in a while

my grandmother would come to visit

with more gifts in her suitcases than clothes

Her footsteps left trails of flowers blooming in her wake

And our home transformed into a greenhouse

of flowers, butterflies, smiles,

and laughter that seemed to sing

How grand it would be to snatch those visits out of the air

and stretch, and tug, and pull them like taffy

Let those moments extend into foreverness

I dreamed of a magic door

that could open in our home

and exit into hers

Whispers of War

Whispers of war began to echo in all our minds

but surely there was nothing to worry about

War is a thing that happens somewhere else

Loss is a thing other people face

So we were sure things would be fine

and drifted off to sleep

It sounded like a crack of thunder and a million bolts of lightning striking our house

I woke up to the window above my head shaking furiously

My sisters trembling in fear nearby

It didn't hit our house, but what did it hit?

Something, maybe someone near us had met their end

Fear took over my mind as I wondered, would I follow them?

And so began our nights huddled on a cold basement floor

hoping to slip by death's gaze

Trying to make ourselves small, and unnoticeable

Sleep did not come to me that first night

And the cold concrete kept me up for many nights after

First

They targeted airports

And hospitals

So those who could leave were trapped

And those who needed help

Couldn't get to it.

And they called *us* the terrorists.

One bomb would drop

And before I could recover from the fear

of the trembling basement walls

hiding myself and the scared eyes of my companions

from the realities above

Another would take its place.

Falling and falling

I was left to imagine a kind of destruction

My young mind was not capable of picturing.

With the sky falling down upon us

What could we do but run?

Your country is at war

You are leaving in 12 hours, you can bring one backpack

What would you put in it?

For me, it was:

The first two chapter books I ever read

Charlotte's Web and *Snot Stew*

–which I had long since outgrown

My CD player with Dido's album *White Flag*

And a golden necklace I've worn since I was 7

It looks like a little flower and has Allah written in calligraphy,

And the opening of the Quran on the back.

Despite my efforts, I couldn't fit my favorite stuffed animals.

I was grasping at straws, trying desperately not to leave my childhood behind,

But by the time we arrived in America, she was dead.

All those goodbyes

With family who did not have the privilege to leave as easily as we could

All those hugs I didn't savor

Not knowing they would be my last

I'd never find my way back to home's embrace

Years would continue to pass

With no consideration for how desperately I wanted to stop time

I would sometimes lose track of which loving set of eyes

Were now buried beneath the ground

How their deaths

Shook the ground half the world away

I wish I had known I would never see them again

Then perhaps I would have had the foresight to remember everything

What they were wearing

What our exact parting words were

How their faces contorted with the mixed emotions of showing

Love and sadness at our departure

But I am not a fortune teller

And I couldn't see the future

The Boat to Cyprus

Within what felt like seconds, the waves I thought would be tranquil

Grew angry and violent

And the faces of my fellow passengers went green.

Once the first person vomited,

there was no hope for the rest of us

It became a domino effect

Of seasickness and dehydration.

The stench of seawater and body fluids—sweat, puke, and who knows what else

Rocked in my belly as I tried for hours

to hold my sickness down.

At some point, I remember being told

To try and reuse bags so we wouldn't run out.

While even the Marines clung on to the sides of the ship for balance, their faces the same shade of green,

There was my mom

Rushing up and down the isles

Helping everyone.

Silent Prayers

It doesn't matter how many times I say *bismillah*
Or how desperately I pray,
I can't stop the bombs from falling,
Nor stop the planes that drop them off
And fly away not caring where they land
If it's a family they're murdering
Or an 11 year old girl's smile
It doesn't matter.
I can't save her.
I can only brace myself as the Earth shakes
Hard enough to mask how hard my lips quiver in fear.
بسم الله الرحمن الرحيم
I can only put my head and heart against the cold stone ground and
pray
That these basement walls don't fall
That the glass doesn't shatter in our sleep.
That my mother's mind isn't lost trying to protect us but
I can't stop those things either.

It doesn't matter how many times I say *bismillah*
Or how desperately I pray,
I can't stop my dad's face from disappearing behind the crowd.
I can't stop the tears rolling down my cheeks
I can't stop my dad's face from disappearing behind the crowd.
I'm at the mercy of the panging in my chest
I can't stop my dad's face from disappearing behind the crowd.
I can't stop the thought that
I will never see my father again.
بسم الله الرحمن الرحيم
I can't stop my feet from climbing on board
Despite how hard I'd try if I could.
To meet a place I've never dreamed of while my dreams lay waste

behind
So many strangers with fear in their eyes
Even the seasickness can't distract us
And I can't help but think
What a nice time for a swim

It doesn't matter how many times I say *bismillah*
Or how desperately I pray,
I can't stop myself from the cold sweats and bad dreams
Or the muffled cries I keep to myself
To stop my mom, who's tired enough, from waking
To comfort her broken child
بسم الله الرحمن الرحيم
The desperate midnight prayers don't help me
I don't know why I bother
With so little space to spare
I can hardly kneel between my air mattress and all the others in the
room I share

It doesn't matter how many times I say *bismillah*
Or how desperately I pray,
So I don't bother anymore.

Originally Published in Muftah Magazine, August 2017

Yearning for Death

Was something I gradually slipped into

With no moment of intense decisiveness.

Instead, it was the little things

That eased me closer to the edge.

All I knew was

By the time I realized

I wanted to take my own life

The idea felt like a warm blanket.

Like home.

But it also felt cold

And alone.

I convinced myself

Going through with it

Was the only way

To stop that coldness from piercing my heart.

Fun fact:

The American Citizen Evacuation of the 2006 Lebanese War was, at the time, the largest evacuation of American citizens in history.

Or in other words, the trauma that made me terrified of death and its permanence,

Simultaneously immortalized me as a member of this historic event.

The thing that made me hypervigilant and fearful for my safety,

Simultaneously made me lust for death.

The events that made me feel profoundly Lebanese,

Marked me permanently as a part of this American history.

Mute Creativity

The words won't come out

They cannot seem to escape the clutches of my teeth

Barring them in like prisoners

I would have liked painting a picture with those words

With colors so bright, their song

Would have been more melodious than that of birds

But I have no paint, no canvas,

And my words are behind iron bars

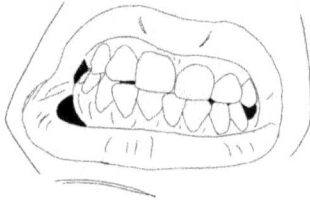

"What's Suicide?"

I asked.

"It's when someone kills themselves," another girl responded.

I was terrified to hear there was a word

For what I had been feeling

And realizing other people felt the same way

How validating to have a word to describe my feelings

And how nightmarish

That enough people never found another answer

For the word to exist in the first place

"I didn't know there was a word for that," I said

"Yeah, it's disgusting.

Only selfish assholes would do something like that," she responded.

Oh. Maybe I really do deserve to die then.

Temper Tantrums

I was always the kid who screamed

When things didn't go my way

Which felt more often than not

I didn't know how to express the pain I felt

over things I didn't know were so meaningless

But I figured if I had to suffer

Why not wreak havoc on the rest of my home too?

Maybe if I cried loud enough someone might hear me

After arriving in America, the tantrums stopped

The temper withered away

Everyone commented on how mature I had gotten

But in actuality

I had no energy left to cry

And everything was worth crying about

Cedar Trees

My first home

My first love

Tasted like naïveté and blind trust

That the world made sense when nothing does

That parents have all the answers

and are immune to fear, and death, and sadness

My memories formed from rock and sand and smiles

Fields of flowers and fresh river water

and happy worms feasting on fruit

But the after-taste

was gunpowder, smog, smoke

and the awakening realization

Life is not a fairy tale

Decisions

I had been living in wishful ignorance

waiting to go home.

Even though all signs told me this was a fool's dream

It wasn't safe yet

I knew that.

School was starting here

I knew that too.

Lebanon would need months to function again

I knew that as well.

And yet I waited for the day my mom might tell us to pack up

my one backpack of items

so that we could go home.

But instead she told us we would stay for a while

Instead she enrolled us in school, and started scouting for apartments

When the realization hit, my heart sank into a sullen place of emptiness

My mind aimlessly raced, with nowhere to go, held down by the gravity of our new circumstances

I thought of the life I once knew and wondered, how long would it take for us to be reunited?

I thought of my family, my father. *When would we see him again? When would he join us? How would he?*

≈

I would go back to this moment in my mind many times for the rest of my life. Realizing that when I thought I understood the "gravity" of staying, I truly had no idea. The rest of my life would be plagued with wonder of what could have been if we *had* gone back, or if we had never left. My mind was occupied with everything but thoughts children should have, as I always wondered what the version of me who got to live in Lebanon her whole life would be like.

There was a fork in the road

Where the path was once clear.

I walked down this path

She walked down the other

And her presence

Haunted me

HAUNTING

Mi amor, when did you get so serious?

Transitions

"Did they teach you how to make bombs in Lebanon?"

It was more of an accusation than a question, which was obvious to anyone who watched the words spit free from his mouth. The young girl didn't feel compelled to give him an answer, instead, she sat there, shrinking before her classmates' eyes. At 75 pounds, standing at a tall 4'11", she didn't think she could get any smaller. And yet, she shrunk beneath the gaze of the cold-hearted substitute standing in front of her.

"Her kind are not to be trusted," he said with his finger pointed at her. She felt diseased, crushed under the weight of the pointing and the eyes of her peers that looked so uncertain, "she is a terrorist." Please, God, let me die, she thought.

"Why don't you tell us what you're really doing here? Huh? Who sent you?"

In hindsight, I probably could have said, "Fuck off asshole, I'm 11!" And marched to the principal's office to demand he be removed from the classroom. However, that kind of autonomy was stripped from me when I left my country by boat with my life in a backpack. So, I said nothing. I just sat there taking it, and cut my tiny wrists when I got home.

Here's a little game for you: your country is at war, you are leaving in 12 hours, and you can bring one backpack--what would you put in it?

Welcome to Amerikkka

Why are you so hairy?

You look like a boy

Why aren't you using the boy's bathroom?

She has mustache

Hairy d*ke

She smells like bomb fluids

Terrorist

I hope you get cancer

Your people are cancer

You gonna cry, bitch?

Go back to the desert

Goat fucker

You're Saying نادیا Wrong

What is my name?

Is it how my father says it?

or how my mother says it?

I don't know, but it surely isn't what you insist on calling me

I didn't know how invalidating wearing my name could feel

or how invisible introductions could be,

but I've learned most people don't listen

when I tell them who I am

They instead respond lies told with full confidence

I am pressured into questioning my own memory—

Who am I?

Some of you grace me with your efforts

and force me to say it "right" again and again

until I become aware of how unpleasant any word sounds when you keep saying it

And you wrestle through it with all your might

Reminding me, how much effort it takes for me to be myself

in this land of unkindness

And by the time you get it--almost--right

I've decided my name will never have a home in your mouth.

خبايا الشباب

I'm playing a tug of war

So many multi-Americans have played

Between fitting in with my old home

Or with my new one

They tug back and forth

I am too *halal* for my friends

Too *haram* for my family

And entered a place where I would never fit in with either

Starstruck

Two worlds collided

Sophomore year of high school

A stranger walked by and made a joke

And for no tangible reason,

these strangers decided they were best friends

And pretended they had been friends all along

Both as another joke to confuse people

and because some part of it felt true

I wonder how I would have reacted

If in that moment

The stars bent down and whispered

"You're going to marry him someday"

But as if we had unlocked

A hidden prophecy

From that day forward

We were best friends

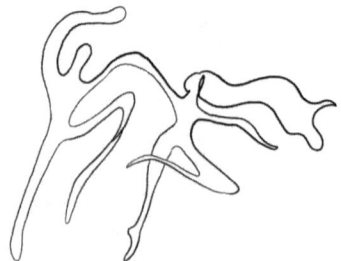

On the last day of school,

the star-sent stranger walked me home

--which we both knew was way out of his way—

And we had a picnic in my apartment complex

Pubescent sweat dripping out all our pores

Wearing hand-me-downs that were too big for us

and still figuring out the right balance of messy hair that still looked cool

but truly, looked disastrous

And I told him everything.

I told him my struggles with self-harm

With suicide

With fitting in

I don't know why I chose to trust him

I just knew when we were together

The fog seemed to clear a bit

The world felt less like it was in greyscale

I felt less like a monster.

I am fascinated

By how kids can be relentlessly bullied

With dumpster-fire mental health

And look upon a new year

or a new school

With excitement for the fresh start it offers

In high school you get to try again

Learn from your middle school mistakes

Turn a page and decide who you want to be this time

And instead of depression or suicide

Maybe you can concern yourself with "normal things"

Like conventional attractiveness

clumsy high school relationships

gossiping and staying out of people's mouths

and the silent unspokenness of

eating disorders, sexual assault

and casual school-shooting drills.

Children are elastic snapping back

clay still molding when they think they may have solidified

Shouldering through chaos while still forming an opinion of the world

The word to describe this phenomena, is resilient.

I am fascinated by the resilience of children.

To the person who reads this,

May your ventures be more fortunate than mine.

I remember my first kiss,

It was by a boy I didn't know from a school I didn't go to

who had followed me home.

He had been watching me.

I was in 7th grade and he was in high school.

I don't remember the first time I had sex,

It was with a man who beat me until I passed out from crying, begging him to stop.

I just remember the bruises on my vagina and the emptiness in my heart.

It was a nightmare I didn't name until years later

Rape.

I do remember the second time, though I wish I could forget.

I thought I was ready to start talking about getting raped.

The first guy I told said if I didn't have sex with him it meant I would never get over my assault

I kept asking him if he was done yet.

"No." He said. "Just relax."

While I cried into a pillow.

～

After I ended things with him, he told everyone I was crazy.

Coerced "consent" is a fancy lie.

Rape.

Or when I became friends with the 38 year old man

I met in rehab after trying to kill myself at 20

He told me he loved me

and stalked me for two years

and every breath of that timespan was occupied

with my constant fear, of

Rape.

I dream of a day when I will not be plagued with violence.

Of a night where I can sleep without screaming.

"What's your biggest fear?"

"Rape"

In the end it didn't matter

that I was someone's daughter

someone's sister

someone's best friend

My "virginity" and below knee-length shorts didn't matter

My reputation as a prude didn't matter

It didn't matter that it was a Tuesday afternoon

With the sun shining bright

It didn't matter that I still met my 8 p.m. curfew that day

All those myths I was told would protect me were lies

Even God couldn't protect me

because in that moment, You were godless

All that mattered was that you chose not to see me for what I am

You chose not to see a person

You chose to see a skin sack of organs,

A mindless, soulless tool

You decided I didn't matter

And you taught me that was the truth

I learned how to act like a bad liar

I left clues to things

I didn't mind them finding out

And sheepishly got nervous

As they followed the wrong trails

So, when I got raped

And came home, laughing and smiling

And played video games with sticky trauma between my legs

And waited until everyone was asleep to scrub my skin raw

No one suspected a thing.

And I've yet to decide

If that was good or bad

I just knew

The secrets weren't so magical anymore.

Death of a Child

I wrote about you in my peacock-feather journal

with gold trim along the pages

(sometimes I forget I was still just a kid)

I bought it with allowance my dad gave me

and told myself I'd only write the most special things

(I bought a pack of smiley-face
stickers to decorate the pages)

I wrote my favorite jokes and funny stories from school

I wrote about things I learned and movies I watched

(sometimes I forget I was still just a kid)

And then I wrote about you and how you broke my heart

and then I wrote about you and how you broke my body

(those words were not as pretty as
the peacock-feather pages)

In a panic I tore out the pages

scared that someone might see them

(I didn't feel like a kid anymore)

~

I thought about throwing it but realized

the wind might blow it out of the trash and into someone's hands

(I wonder if they'd think the pages were pretty)

I thought, if I tear it, someone might piece it back together

If I burn it, someone might smell the smoke

(I didn't feel like a kid anymore)

I hyperventilated and ate the pages

And hoped the ink would kill me with it

(I guess I wasn't a kid anymore)

I wrote about you, and then I stopped writing.

Magnolia Flower

Beautiful, polluted, pink sunsets

as deceptive as the hospitable smiles

The home

where I always felt alone

The food so good it's celebrated like a God

The people so free they dance

through drive-through daiquiris

that never felt quite inviting to me

The murderous rains and vengeful pests

That fed on my flesh

While people drowned me with roars

"Go back where you came from

you sand-n-word-whore"

The small-town vibes

Where everyone knows everything

and still, no one cares

and your rapist still has 32 mutual friends

Who must be aware.

Cutting

Something about the control over my own body

Felt like ecstasy

I liked the secrecy of it

I liked the sight of my blood

I liked the feeling of my wounds sticking to my pants

I like the adrenaline, and how it allowed me to feel like a person

I had this secret no one knew about

and no one could do a thing to stop me

I wanted that control

But the more I did it

the more I realized I had no control anymore

My body moved without instruction

I felt nothing but fear that if I didn't cut, I'd die

if I didn't cut, I'd do something worse than cutting

Cutting wasn't ecstasy, it was air

Someone had been holding my head underwater

and with the sight of red, I could breathe again

A wave of relief followed by sickening shame

The more I hated myself, the more I wanted to hurt myself

Dreamer

There's a gentle humming in my ear

The sound not unfamiliar

And I think I've seen you in my dreams,

The ones resembling nightmares.

After all, how could I forget how sweetly you sang my names,

Gorgeous, Sweetheart,

Cunt & Lying Whore

Or how sweetly the scent of your neck mixed with the saltiness of my tears,

How could I forget the soft caress of your hand whacking the back of my head

Insisting

"You wanted this."

Tell me my darling, who were you trying to convince?

You never graced me with your smile again,

Or your frown, your laugh or fist.

I found myself wondering if you were even real

Or a myth I made up instead.

If you were the incubus in my bed

Or just the screaming in my head.

~

But every night I go to dream

And see you standing there,

As a ghoul, devil or fiend.

So many different faces, but I always know it's you

because they all look at me just as sweetly,

as the night you ruined me, then threw me away.

The loving look of hatred and disgust that you've printed on my eyelids

So your eyes are there every time I close mine.

And I can't tell who I disgust more

If it's my darling or if it's me.

You were right to disappear,

you had everything to hide.

I only wish you could've seen how desperately I cried.

I only wish you could have answered the questions drowning in my mind

"Do you even know what you did?"

"Did you *really* think I wanted it?"

"Should I have resisted harder?"

Cool metal traces where your fingerprints have been,

I remember every part you touched

And watched it go from purple, to skin, to red.

∾

And I can't get myself to scream

"Stop."

And I can't get myself to answer

Who I'd be screaming to,

You or the blade?

You took some parts of me with you

 but I won't need them where I'm going.

I just need to close my eyes and keep dreaming until the horrors finally end

There were no flowers for me

Or get-well-soon cards.

Only silence.

Only shame.

Enough of each to echo back and forth between my ears

And make sure that this is a place

I never get to leave.

But that's okay.

I'll see you in my dreams.

Wilted Roses

Before my eyes, a wilted rose lay in disbelief

her cheeks, once radiant and sunkissed--

were pallid, grey

the echo of her last laughs

a ghost in the room

and everything else, carted away by strangers

in a zipped black sack.

Tears welled in my eyes like acid

and rage choked my heart

as guilt began to creep in my mind

prodding at all the ways

I could have loved her better.

The last petal floated elegantly to the ground

seemingly unaware that all the air had left the room

and left us to squander with the tidbits of hope we latched onto

it lingered purposelessly in the room until it, too

Wilted.

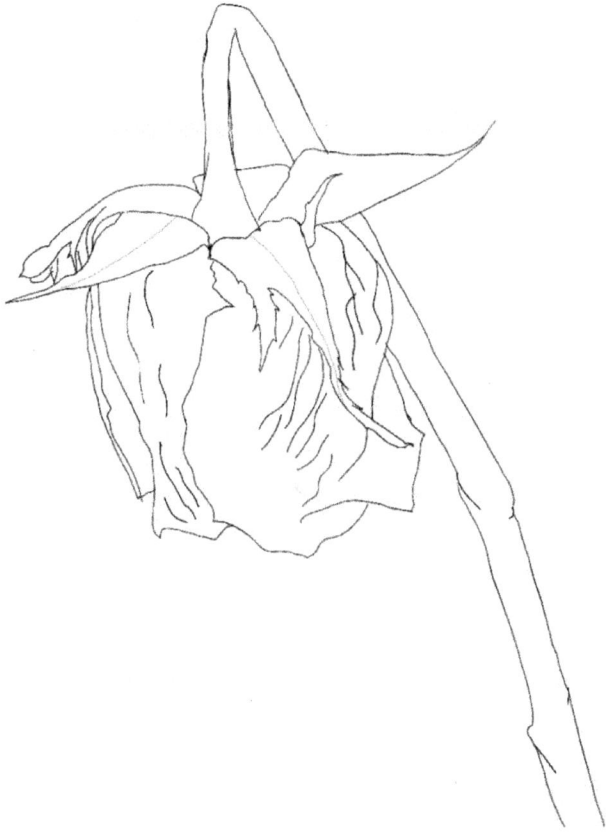

Unholy Trinity

Depression, Anxiety, and PTSD

i. Depression

Am I floating, drowning, sinking?

Time has become the muted sound of water in my ears

From how long I have been anchored to the bottom of the sea.

The sea monsters swim in slow motion around me

And bottom feeders won't feast on my flesh

They don't want to be filled with my poison.

Everything is slow.

Cold.

Heavy.

And there is no way to the surface.

There is a cave in my chest where a black hole has formed

Expanding the chasm of cold, infinity into oblivion

While in my hands the shriveled remains lay, of the heart that simply

Stopped beating.

The circles under my eyes are darker than this pit I am imprisoned in.

I can't breathe beneath these waters

ii. Anxiety

I am immersed in flames

Embers searing my flesh and all my veins pop out

I am forgetting or I am failing

But something is not right

I can feel my pulse in my neck

My heart clenches, tenses, and I don't know for what

But there is a reason for my eyes to be so bloodshot

Something is coming or something isn't working

Or someone is watching me or something is going wrong

But something is not right

I am breathing too quickly and I can't breathe

iii. PTSD

Shrouded by smoke and smog and mist and fog

I can hardly see my fingertips

The clouds hug around my waste in such a way

That I too, become a ghost

Surrounded by unforgiving eyes of

You, and you, and you.

If only it was just the eyes who followed me wherever I go

And though I whisper that you aren't real

you creep into my dreams

And though I push you from my mind

I still live in fear

of hands still tugging on my hair

of hands latching around my throat

The words "please" "stop" floating dryly in the air

Another ghost, lingering

And

I can't breathe with your hand around my neck.

"What's been going on with you?"

Rape was just a thing that happened

To loose women in short skirts

Walking home alone when it's too dark

Who ran into the wrong stranger.

With that mythological definition as the only truth I knew

How could it possibly define what happened to me?

How could I even begin reaching out to that hand,

desperately trying to help me?

I remember swallowing pills

And falling asleep

Not quite sure if I had taken enough

If the sleep was the release of death

or the fatigue of my tears lulling me into unconsciousness

But when I woke, everything was the same

Weeks went by without a smile

Months went by with no feelings

Just numbness in my chest

Occasionally visited by hopelessness and despair

And for a while I was certain

I had died and gone to hell

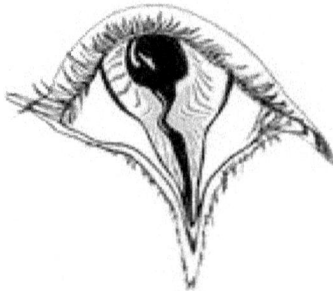

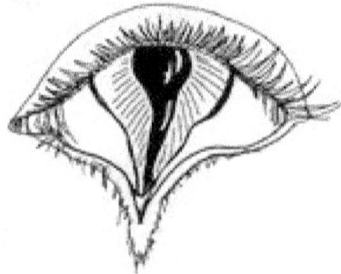

I saw you crying over my hospital bed,

that time I tried to kill myself

and ended up in the psych division instead

I got dragged out of a therapist's office in handcuffs

after police inappropriately patted me down

shoved me to the back of their car

all for saying I needed help.

They made me take some medicine,

they didn't tell me what it was

the woman next to me was strapped to her bed

and screamed all night

I was naked but for the hospital gown

on a hard, cold bed

and I couldn't keep my eyes open from fatigue.

But I heard your stifled cries,

I opened my eyes and saw you

sitting at the foot of my bed

sobbing with your hands covering your face

thinking you might choke on your tears

and die right before my eyes.

∾

I wanted to reach out and comfort you,

but I didn't know what to say

so I pretended I was still asleep

and all I could think

was that you deserved a better kid than me.

The Storm

It was raining when I was born

So hard, my father could not see in front of his car

He had no choice but to keep going forward

Windshield wipers raging on

And on, and on

And surviving on the faint hope that no one else was on the road

And he was already ready

To die for me

Before I took my first breath

I was already in a debt I could never repay

And it got higher every time he smiled at me

With all the warmth in his heart

I felt a shiver in my spine because I knew

I never deserved a father like him

Disappointment was written in my stars

And tattooed in my veins

Pumping through me like a disease with no hope for a cure

Injected in the storm that brought me into this world

I inherited your bad luck, *baba*

And every time lightning struck

It struck me further from you

Phantom

There are times I look in the mirror

And I still feel dirty

Or I'll catch myself zoning out—I got distracted

By some dumb shit

And forgot to stop myself from thinking about it

So I shoot back to that moment—

That one detrimental moment

That even though I say—

—and they all agree—

that it doesn't define me, it does.

And I start to cry.

Why else would I have to so carefully

Monitor my thoughts

24 hours a day

7 days a week

52 weeks a year

for 4 years now

to avoid slipping into it

If not because its monstrosity

Redefined me

～

I look at myself, and I feel disgusting.

I *am* disgusting.

I'm disgusting, I'm DISGUSTING.

The things that have happened to my body, are disgusting

And I will never get a new body

I'm stuck reliving the torment every time

I take my clothes off I see the bruises

That have long since faded away,

But are tattooed in my mind where he left them.

When I can even bear to look at myself

I don't see a person anymore, all I see is

Pain Pain Pain Pain Pain.

And fear.

A gentle hand feels like a threat

A claw to choke me with

To shove my face into a pillow

Until it feels like I'm dying and I wish I was dead

So the memory can't complete itself

They say I'm strong

Even though there's nothing left of me to be strong.

Dead R*pe Baby

I couldn't decide what you were

a cluster of bastardous cells,

or something more than that

If culture or logic would win over my reasoning,

I would have aborted you anyway.

But God spared my poor soul

and decided that you were not my destiny.

Still, I wondered

how come I have to grapple this demon

and wear you as another trauma?

Another smear on my dirty window

Another fracture on my broken soul,

while he gets to forget me

and all that he did to me?

Still, I wondered

Why the tears? Was I grieving? Did I care about you?

Or were the tears from something else?

From the awareness that my body had irrevocably betrayed me by
carrying you?

By making me find out like this?

~

Or were they from exacerbation that I couldn't just "Move On?"

and be done with this whole ordeal?

Were they from shame?

I had a lot of shame. There was probably some shame.

Whatever the tears were about,

I looked down at you—mangled mass of bloody cells—

With a surprising emptiness in me

clouding the deep echoes of rage and grief

At the terror, realizing he had never left me until this moment.

The realization that my body, was not *my* body.

I flushed you down the toilet in an unceremonious goodbye.

Hastily hiding the evidence.

I don't know what the right thing to do is for this situation.

Your ghost,

Haunts me too.

A single tap

On a traumatized soul

Can cause it to spiral

Into madness

I am a glass cannon on a runaway train

Of unexplainably bad decisions

One bump in the road and I shatter into shards of shrapnel and spikes of glass

splintering the skin of all my fellow passengers

and yet the train spirals along

It misplaced its brakes long ago

and I only hope if it goes fast enough it might glide over the bumps

Somehow I may not shatter to dust

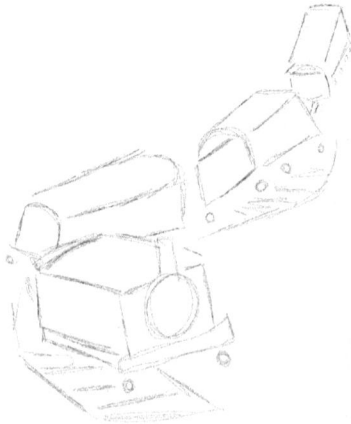

Your memory lingered

Like stubborn second-hand smoke

No scrubbing seems enough to rid the walls of my memory

Of the dingy, yellow stains you left behind.

And I ooze putrid thoughts of you

Through pus-filled holes in my soul that weren't there before you.

Everyone can see my flesh is rotten,

Through watery eyes as they choke on my stench

They stay away, desperately holding their breath.

I reek of your rancid memories,

And this is what you smell like.

I've tried to feed off people

Like a parasite

Trying to fill the unquenchable hunger

That burns in my stomach like acid

The thirst that leaves my mouth dry and lips cracked

The desperation

For *someone* to love me.

But no matter what I do

I can't even get them to look at me

Like I'm something less than parasitic.

Just, unimportant.

Lost in Translation

Like a poem, I've gotten lost in translation

And a part of me withers away overseas

As I struggle to be understood

By people who are speaking English,

But an entirely different language.

And my voice gets washed out by the volume

Of people who think they're more important than me.

When I scream I am unheard

When I beg I am mocked

and made to believe the fault must be with me

I must be misconveying something

or I *must* be misunderstanding someone

--and all their "good intentions."

I fight, but

Too often I find myself in a world that doesn't fight for me.

Like a poem

مثل قصيد

I've gotten lost in translation.

لقد ضعت في اتفسير

I can't stop moving

Doing

Creating

If I stop I might think

If I think, I might think of you

If I think of you

I might think of what you did to me

And if I think of what you did to me

I might think I am a broken worthless idiot

So I can't stop moving

I have to keep proving

To myself

To everyone else

That I have value

I am exhausted

I am fatigued

I have to keep making things

And doing things

That make people say

"She's awesome"

Or

"She's badass"

❧

or

"She does so much for other people"

Anything to satisfy that need for love

That I do not get from myself

That I do not get at home

That I crave with more intensity than a meth addiction

To prove that I am not a broken person

Even if the strain this exhaustion sets on my heart

Kills me

• • • Breaks are for mentally healthy people• • •

The all-consuming fear

Of being hurt again

Made me shudder at the sight of my own shadow

Afraid she may reach out to strangle me

And believe even the air in my lungs may betray me

And slip out

Leaving me to choke

And gasp

And claw for my life that would not return

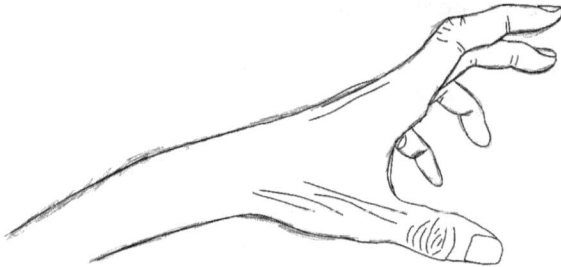

Ghost Stories

My heart has sunk into the depths of the universe

Wrestling demons I've failed to forget

I am a ghost

Ravaging the lands in a swarm of gloom

So others can't feel the warmth of the sun

That fails to kiss my translucent skin

Yet any combination of words could

Exercise my fragile existence

And send my small spirit from the
cave it rests in,

From the cavity in my chest,

Into some other plane of existence

Someplace, maybe worse than here.

Part of me invites it,

A smaller part, weeps at the invitation.

They Are Still Abusing You

Forgive and forget

The rhetoric sung by abusers

For generations

How clever to convince people

The only way to know peace

Is to stop carrying hate in your heart

But how can peace exist

If you are cut

And let them keep the knife

They used to harm you?

The earth is angry

She has been hurt

So she sets fires to the lands

We claim are ours

And floods us out of homes

We never earned

While the ground trembles beneath our feet

And the sky falls above our heads

I am the earth

I've been walked on

Abused

Used

Mistreated

And I've had men in suits

Decide my pain isn't real

And if they told the earth

To calm down

She would laugh

And split the ground beneath their feet

Eating them alive

∿

Like the earth, I fight back

And make my misery uninhabitable for you

Once you are gone

Like vines breaking through concrete roads

My smile will return

As my resurrection begins.

RESURRECTING

I break through the ground with dirt caked beneath my nails,
ready to walk again

I thought I didn't belong there anymore

But I've realized now,

It's just your version of the world

I don't belong to.

My Lebanon is the place where people can be who they want.

Where diversity is a point of pride

& women are free to be what they want

and wear what they want

My Lebanon has a history as deep as the sea

And a future as bright as the sun

Because—even if it is a slow process—

My Lebanon is a place that progresses.

I don't want my life to be defined

By anger, and pain, and resentment.

Though I've been blamed for those things, it hasn't been one-sided.

Part of me wants to write a laundry list

Of all the ways you've hurt me

But it's a small part

The part that hasn't yet learned how to let go.

The bigger part of me understands what I'm letting go of--

Years of repressing my beautiful, chaotic nature

And replacing them with fake smiles

While my real smiles hid behind locked doors

You didn't care to open.

So I am letting go of the pain

Of never being good enough

And never being allowed to be myself

I am letting go of the rejection, of being mocked, and ignored.

Those mistakes you made don't haunt me anymore

And with that, you don't haunt me either.

I am happy,

And I hope you can one day

Make enough peace with your demons to see it.

What eyes do you use to see me,

And are you as unkind with yourself?

Which flaws do you see in me,

That make my happiness seem like I only exist

To be a mockery of you?

What eyes do you use for your reflection?

And do you weep at the sight?

It is a pain I am familiar with

But I have learned to be gentle

With myself, and with you

You may try to tear me down

And lash at my throat to silence me

But when I weep, it is not from pain

Or fear that you have any power over me

I weep at the glimpse of what it is to be you

What a weight to carry

When joy is a threat and anger is safe

And you hate because you hate yourself

I weep because you're hurting too

～

I hope you find the courage to see yourself

With gentle eyes

But for now, I'll close mine

When I'm writing poems

I hear your voice in my head

Invalidating me

And I question every stroke of my pen

Wondering, if you read this, what will you think?

What holes will you pick out and burn into my skin?

Which of my words will be used against me?

And I feel small and afraid and unmotivated

And embarrassed and ashamed

And and and

And question my memory and question my truths

And question my purpose and question my feelings

And and and

And in the end I am so tiny

And feel I am being watched beneath a microscope

each part of me picked at and prodded

But I keep writing

Until my voice is louder than your shame

Español

Quiero escribir una poema en español
Pero no puedo
Quiero leo los palabras de mis antepasadas
Pero ellos no me conocen
Cuando pienso que quiero escribir
Estoy asustada

No tengo casa en español
No tengo mi abuela o mi tia
Ellas viven con Dios
Y no se si pueden escucharme cuando hablo

Mi español es malo
Es peor que mi árabe
Entonces escribo en ingles
Un idioma que no tiene hogar

English

I want to write a poem in spanish
But I can't
I want to read the words of my ancestors
but they don't know me
When I think I might want to write
I am afraid

I don't have a home in spanish
I don't have my grandmother, or my aunt
They live with God
And I don't know if they can hear me when I speak

My spanish is bad
It's worse than my arabic
So I write in english
A language that doesn't have a home

I Am Enough

For years I played the tug of war

So many multi-Americans play

Between finding peace in a new home

Or clinging on to the homes of my past

Existing in a lonely cultural limbo

And often feeling homeless

People don't fit so easily into the boxes we make for ourselves

We aren't a one-size-fits-all

While much of me yearns for a place to fully fit in

Where everyone is just like me

Thinks like me

Acts like me

Feels like me

I don't have to choose an identity so that I can belong

I've learned to love myself as I am

Too western for the east, too eastern for the west

And I've decided, I do belong in each of these spaces

Because no one can tell me who I am

Or decide if I am enough

That is a decision I make for myself

Mirror

I often wonder of the stories my wrinkles tell

Wrinkles I'm too young to have

Yet feel like I've been born with

If you look closely

You can see the number of times I've screamed and cried

Imprinted on my face like I was branded by my pain

But there are new lines forming around my eyes

where the whispers of recent smiles

have made their presence known

And remind me that there's still plenty of time

for my wrinkles to tell a multifaceted story

of pain and hurt and joy and life

I am reminded that I am not dead yet

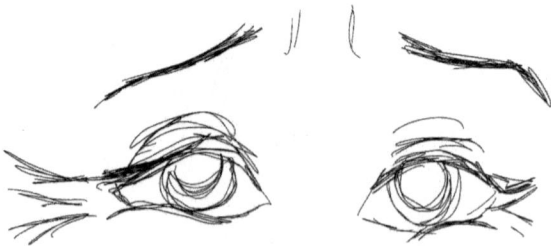

I thought you'd run away

When you saw me without my mask

I had worn it for so long

I forgot the porcelain smile I was known for

Was so far from the truth

But you stayed

Even when I thought I was unlovable

You showed me how wrong I was

Spirituality

Trauma made my faith stronger

—I was still alive after all

Trauma made my faith weaken at its core

—but how did God let this happen?

Both of us grew uncertain of each other

—my spirituality and me—

She feared she had hurt me

I feared I had failed her

We tiptoed around each other anxiously

With a yearning to be whole

And fears of what that confrontation might mean

As with all relationships, my trust felt broken

Trust in God, trust in myself,

I pushed you away and in your absence

I felt emptiness

a pain deeper than pain, a loneliness more hollow

I was scared to reach back out,

scared there wouldn't be a hand waiting for my return

Scared you might drop me

～

I see the ways you've followed me, letting me know

When I am ready you'll still be here, loving me

Giving me the things I deserve, the things I need in this world

Guiding me to the strength I needed to build those things for myself

And my heart is open again

وهو معكم أين ما كنتم
And he is with you wherever you are
Quran 57:4

Body and Spirit

I don't remember it happening

I don't remember *being* assaulted

There were no drugs involved that I was aware of

But my soul lifted from my body

and decided I didn't need to see what happened next

I felt myself float away from that space

far enough where I could no longer see myself

and when I came back, frozen and uncertain

my body took over

walk

she reminded me

one foot in front of the other

keep walking

keep walking

k e e p w a l k i n g

My limp spirit cradled in my body's arms

She showed me how strong she was

When we don't talk about things

like sex or assault

we create a void of silence

where survivors' fears echo around

I was worried I was broken

I was worried I was a bad Muslim

I was worried I was *no longer* Muslim

I was worried he had raped the Arab out of me

I had never heard of a respectable Arab getting raped

(Rape was just a thing that happened to loose women in short skirts)

I was worried I was *eib*

I was worried the essence of my being was now *haram*

I was worried I'd never find love

I was worried no one would ever want to touch me again

(because I was a dirty, broken thing)

I was worried I'd never want to be touched again

In the silence we create with stigma, I lived alone with all my fears

So don't tell me not to write

Don't tell me not to scream my pain from a rooftop

∾

It's not for you

I write to free myself from that prison of isolation

I write so if someone is reading this

in that space of fear and darkness

They will know, it wasn't their fault

And they will know,

They are not alone

You were the beginning of the end

The first nightmare

In a series of bad dreams

But you could not keep me there

• • **Awake** • •

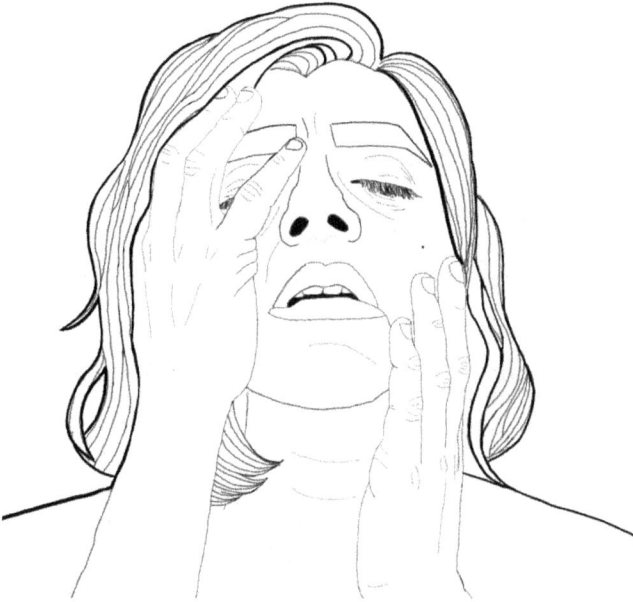

Solidarity

My resurrection was not an art done in isolation

rather varying forms of sisterhood

coaxed me out of the fortress I had built for myself

with their gentle, "me too's"

It was the intimacy of anger

shared among powerful women who had felt fear

and became fearless

The realization that we were not alone

(and the desperate wish that we were)

because it's easier to imagine a world where sexual assault is an isolated incident

instead of something all my friends had experienced

in one way or another

Still, I saw that hopelessness wasn't the only answer

And was guided somewhere on the scale

between passion, and anger

where I began to find my own peace

Aspens and Snow

The dry mountain air, a reminiscent relic of my childhood

And everything else, a reminder

that I cannot build a time machine

And mountains won't make me belong

where I no longer do, or never did.

They're overshadowed by the gargantuan beast

That is a lifetime of uncertainty, self-consciousness, self-doubt

And the desire to be so small, that I am invisible.

You were my hopes and dreams

that my diaspora was an external fiend

and in your arms, I learned that I deeply needed help

Despite the racism and isolation your lands reaped

I left feeling like I left my home behind

hoping to one day see my old friend again

Thank you, for the hope you instilled in my heart

that maybe I am capable of belonging

in a world where I don't fit in.

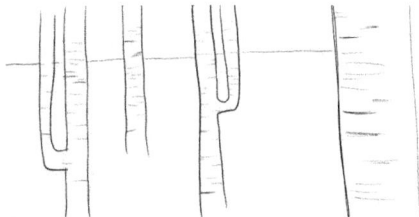

To my Past Lives

I wish I could keep you

But as I hold you in my hands

I can see your petals fluttering away

One by one

A flower wilting with the changing seasons.

With time new blossoms will sprout from the same vines

But although we look the same,

It's only a passing resemblance for anyone who truly knew

So I know I can't keep you, not forever.

Not the version of you who so badly needed love

Not the you who needed strength

Though I want to bring you with me it seems we can't exist in the same space

As I feel the warmth of the sun on my skin, the coldness of your touch seems like a distant nightmare

But I will carry your memories with me

And spread your ashes in the wind

Witches and Fiends

I would turn you into a pig

but you were born that way

I'd have my lions feast on your flesh

but they smell rott from miles away

How I'd revel at the stains on my hands

from herbs used to poison you

But Aeaea's no place for rapists to rest

so I'd sooner watch you drown

And my eyes will mold you to stone

by the curses put on me

from all the cruel Athenas

who blamed me for your deceit

I will rewrite my story with your remains

And take my lions for walks

in my garden of statue graves

How confusing it is

To be so many things

In a world

Only designed for one type of person

But while you may be a planet

I am the universe

And I don't need you to make space for me

For I have made infinite space for myself

Did you see how strongly I wanted to be held by you?

You must have known

When you finally pulled me in for a hug

And kissed my hair

It shot down my spine like an electric bolt

And bounced back up to my heart

Where it has rested ever since

I came to you

With broken glass

Shards of my shattered life

Poking through my bleeding skin

Hands outstretched I pleaded

"I don't know what to do with this"

You took me to a canvas

And I made it a mosaic

Beneath the scabs where I've been

burned and butchered—I change

I am born again in fire with a strength unfamiliar

Again, I am beaten and abused. Again, I am ash.

Again, I rebuild.

And shed old skins like bad dreams of yesterday

I am torn between lives

And no eyes look like my own

I do not recognize her sadness

I do not recognize her joy

Yet I hold on, afraid if I let go

Their pain will wither into dust

Forgotten in the wind

A voice that was once familiar to me whispers,

I do not need these old scales

Let go and know the body is changed

But these hands are yours

And this joy too may fade

And beneath the scabs

You will emerge again.

Marigolds and *Ofrendas*

There are waves of guilt and sadness

That I didn't love you enough while you were living

and I doubt you would have believed this

But you have crossed my mind every single day since you left us

I keep your memory alive in my heart and in my home

with pictures, and flowers, and foods

tres leches and *pan dulce*

Tasted sweeter with you here

my *tortillas* and *tamales*

are so poorly made you'd laugh

And I tell stories about you to my love

So he can feel like he knows you

And I wish I could have introduced you two

giggled with you about how cute he is

when he wasn't around to hear our smiles

Wish I could have shared tears of joy with you

On my wedding day

instead of just wearing your jewels

But I find the ways to feel you with me,

And you are *always* with me.

The biggest lie ever told

Is that you must forgive those who've wronged you

To be free

I forgave my first rapist

Though I hope it brought him peace,

It didn't stop the night terrors

From strangling me in my sleep.

The forgiveness wasn't *for* me.

So, I've decided I'm not a forgiving person

I will hold on to my anger

Until you deserve to be free

From the clutches of your guilt.

My right to be angry

Is what sets me free

My pain is valid, my rage is tangible.

And when I held my ground

And forced you to confront what you did

I breathed for the first time.

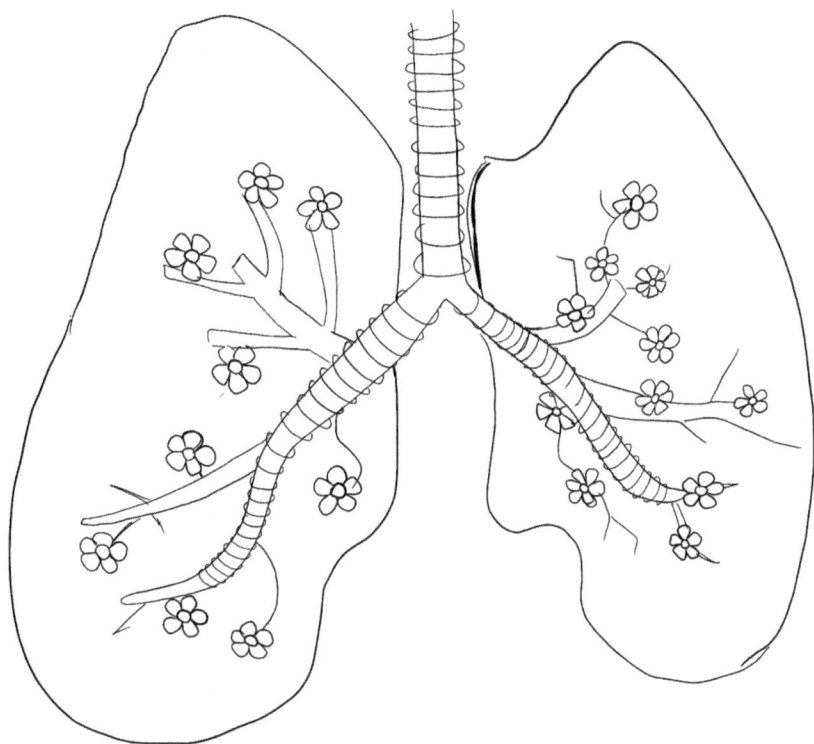

BREATHING

I am breathing and the air is toxic

Revisiting Nightmares

You have 12 hours.

You are fleeing your home.

You can bring one backpack.

What would you put in it?

I obsessed over the question,

the scenario,

the materialistic attachments.

I became accustomed to planning out exactly what outfits I would want to take

and which of my belongings were okay to leave behind.

Every few years I'd ask myself,

What's in the backpack?

But after I fell in love,

I realized it didn't matter what was in the backpack

as long as he was coming with me.

The sadness still comes in waves

Like clouds of fog

Reminding me of my burns

And scars

But I've learned to navigate the haziness

Through the pains of memories

I wake

And grieve all the losses and betrayals.

But I don't carry the pain anymore

I just visit it from time to time.

Love-Letter to my Mental Health

There is an expectation

That "healing" is a concrete thing

A finish line you cross

When suddenly you're

"better."

This may be true for some people

And the process of realizing I was not one of those people

Was disheartening on good days

And soul-crushing on bad ones

There are weeks when I feel great

And there are weeks I can't get out of bed

But being hard on myself never helped

So instead I choose to love myself

When I'm too depressed to shower

When I'm too depressed to speak or open my eyes

When the dishes pile up

And I run out of clean clothes

When even a grain of rice is too much for me to stomach

∿

When I'm so anxious I can't breathe

When I talk myself down from countless panic attacks

And find myself snapping my neck to look over my shoulder

Making sure no one's following me

When I get so stressed I pick my skin raw

And pluck my eyebrows until they're swollen, bleeding,

and criminally mismatched

All because I forgot my fidget toys at home

When my mind runs wild with every possible worst-case scenario

I crumble into despair and uncontrollable tears

Feeling the pain as if it was real

In those moments, I choose to love myself.

On the good days, and the bad,

I choose to love myself.

If you told me I'd reach a point,

Where more of my tears

Were from joy than pain

I would have laughed at your words

and known how wrong they were

I used to cry myself to sleep each night

Like a ritual to cleanse myself

From the burdens of each day

Joy was but a fleeting glimmer of light

in a cavern that was otherwise cloaked with darkness

Yet here I stand

Strong, Content

Capable of loving myself and others

Without the weight of resentment holding me back

On most days,

I am Happy.

Dear body of mine,

It hurts to think of how I've abused you

That my response to wounds from others

Was to inflict even more pain on myself

And you've turned into the strongest metals

To keep me standing upright

When all my insides felt like poisoned liquids

Ready to spill out

You were my shell

When I scarred myself you showed me

Even the deepest scars can heal

When there was no energy left in my spirit

You kept walking forward

And I've learned the joy

Of loving every inch of you

As if you were the sun itself

Gardens in the Afterlife

In my dream I saw you

I had been running

From the same darkness that haunts me

Suffocating in the cloak of fear

I've gotten so accustomed to wearing

Ghosts surrounding me, screaming at the top of their hollow lungs

In my dream I clutched my ears and shut my eyes

Determined to wake up

And I felt a sudden peace, a quietness

I opened my eyes and saw you

Dressed more fashionably than me

With your hair sitting in perfect white curls

Beneath your sun hat

We were surrounded by fields of flowers

glowing in the sunlight

all craving your attention, as if you were their Queen

You held me and told me not to be afraid

and said you were always here to protect me

And I woke in blissful tears

Happy to have seen you again

Where does your life begin?

For me it wasn't at birth

But at the first bomb drop

I died

And I was born, yanked into another dimension

Everything before then feels an irrelevant, distant dream

As a pillar crumbled and created a fork in the road where the path was once clear.

What was once a whole person

diverged into differing timelines

As I walked down this path, and she walked down the other

I think of her often

Dead and in the ground of my timeline, does she thrive in hers?

I wonder if she could gaze at this version of her future

would she like me--or gasp at the sight?

She had a strong bite

And the same stubbornness as me

So, I wonder, how much of me exists in her?

How much of her exists in me?

Although our lives have been different—how much of who I am existed, before the trauma did?

∾

I look back and think of the girl

who only I knew

The girl who fiercely stood up for herself

especially when the odds were not in her favor

The girl whose tears were frequent and heavy

and who never quite felt she belonged

Who got knocked down time and time again

And always stood up

And I know, we would have gotten along.

Forests ablaze in unforgiving embers

with cities shrouded in black smoke, smog, charcoal raining down

And rapists are given empathy

With victims, blamed and shamed

And children are dying on streets

With no roof to call their own

And children are dying in their mothers' arms

With no food to eat

And children are dying in oceans

Desperate to reach a dream of safety

And children dying from bombs

Raining down as inescapable as sunshine

Limbs scattered, hearts are Pollock paintings on the ground

And women are cut with rusty knives

With infections spreading from our clits to our hearts

We are second-class citizens of this world

People of color are bleeding everywhere

While eyes turn away, fixated on dollar signs

but help is an unprofitable field

so help is left to us

who are fatigued from all this

bleeding

Penmanship

The nameless boy washed along the shore

didn't survive the raft not meant to overcome oceans

it was made of an ink that bled into the ocean and left him stranded.

This boy could have been my father.

The nameless girl locked in a cage after trying to reach safety

raped, sitting in her own waste

was told promises of safety written in an ink

that wrapped around her beaten wrists like shackles

this girl could have been my mother.

Everywhere my people bleed

as we trek a world built for crueler souls

when we were map makers, we could not see this future

not written in stars but written in blood taken from our veins

and used as an ink that cannot be erased

We are a body count glistening in the moonlight

The air in our lungs is an accident, a coincidence

And you ask me if I am happy.

I look at thos words written in my cousin's blood and question what
happiness is.

Our Legacy

We carry the names

of our uncles and aunts

and all their violent deaths

knowing their last moments

were lived in fear

Is our legacy nothing but fear,

and piles of bodies so high

the sun is shadowed by their volume?

What can we do but thankfully sip our tea

knowing that death has not yet chosen us

knowing that when it is our turn

he will not let us go peacefully

For what do we do to seek forgiveness a from the world of people

that will never forgive us for drawing a breath as Arabs

and still smiling, and loving,

as if our very beating hearts were a revolution

against all tyrants that would rather see us

crying in the mud, dirt caked onto our skin

∾

But instead we build houses in this world that remembered us first

We dance, we marry, we love,

and we name our children

after our aunts and uncles who died violently

not for the fear in their hearts in their final moments

but for the rebellion their very lives carried

and the bravery they had for us.

We refuse to be walked on.

That is our legacy.

Breathing is

a balancing act of hope and disillusionment

with fire scorching all around

I breath, but the air is poison in my lungs

and step out of my skin to see that we are all burning

But in the eye of the storm

at the center where the winds halt

I have carved out a space in this chaotic world

where the tides don't crash so violently

and the shrapnel doesn't breach my skin

I cast a spell where peace and contentment

exist unscathed

I am learning to reach into the smog for a hand and pull you--

whoever you may be--into a safer place too

With a dream that we may all find peace

One day

Climbing

I can't rest simply because "I" have reached peace

it is a fragile illusion while others bleed

susceptible to crack in unsafe hands

There is no rest until we all find the tranquility of freedom,

equality,

and power.

As you climb, view your haven as a place to recharge

not retreat

don't pull up the ladder behind you

but ponder the ways each step higher

is an increase of your volume

leverage

and reach

and how you may use old scars as a reminder

as you move in these new spaces

knowing that problems don't disappear with your individual experience

and there is still work to do

until we all know the feeling

of breathing in safety

and exhaling peace.

Cherry Blossoms in the City

Walking along sidewalks

Of familiar faces in a

little-big city where

everyone is too busy for each other

and nature is so far away

As is the rest of the world.

In that loneliness there is the knowledge

The cherry blossoms will bloom in spring

And the city will breath with all its lungs

Walking together

going--who knows where?

Here is the world and all its people

When they bloom

They bring hope, excitement, rebirth

And a reminder that even the longest winters end.

Fragmented blisters of myself fall back into place

And all the timelines converge

until one day I realize

I am whole

and have always been whole.

Even when I felt most shattered

across different dimensions of myself

I was never broken

There was never anything "wrong" with me

I never needed to change who I was

and I come back to myself now

Fully embracing the good and ugly

with the courage to be who I have always been

Me.

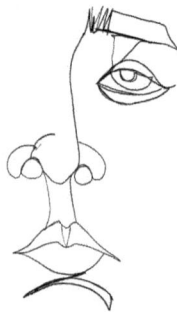

Storm clouds part and I realize

I am a lot like my parents

Emotional, insecure, explosive at times

But I am lucky to have inherited their resilience too

I have my dad's lame sense of humor and my mother's general tastes

And those things make the dates taste sweeter

When we eat them together

And all the tea leaves seem more fragrant

I honor myself and my ancestors through them

For they are the gateway to my history

The map to my past and present selves

And we have moved to a point where

I feel their love again

And this time it doesn't hurt

And this time, it doesn't scare me.

We are one

You are as much a part of my own being

As the hands that write this

As the beating heart in my chest.

When we lay with our limbs entangled

I can't tell where I end and where you begin

And in those moments

I feel safe.

When you smile

My spine turns to warm honey

And my lungs are filled with ocean breeze

Your laughter tastes like the sunset

And your gaze bears the reminiscent scent

Of honeysuckle

Jasmine flowers

the bark of cedar trees

And the heat of the sun on my cheeks

All of which remind me

That I'm not as old as I feel

Saltwater in the Sky

Growing up multi ethnic left me with the feeling

that I was always failing

Someone, somewhere, would think

I was not enough

Starting this love I worried

I was reviving the skeletons in my closet

and would dilute myself further into nothingness

Which was how I often felt

Bargaining with identity

how could I authentically love who I am

If I was always deciding

Which parts of me could be kept, which wouldn't fit this romance

between the ocean and the sky

Our love has lost me nothing

but the fear that I was unworthy

and the self conscious voices that once told me

I was too complicated to be loved as I am

With you, nothing has been a sacrifice

but an exercise in joining two different things together

～

We merge and dance on the ocean

as we swim in the clouds

and create something more magical than miracles

My language rolling off your tongue lulls me into a dream

as sweet as falling in love again in the language of my people
has been

and we are building a home

big enough for us both to live as ourselves

with no walls to box our identities in

Through my heavy-lidded eyes

I focus on your silhouette being traced

By the single ray of sunlight trickling through the blinds

It's as eager to kiss you "good morning" as I am

The first thing I feel when I wake up

Is my heart beating in my chest

I don't know when spring will come

But I've seen her peak behind the clouds

She's often the shortest season between

The blistering colds and smothering heats

Sometimes she's just a passing hello

But know spring will come

I've seen her peak behind the clouds

And offer her sanctuary to my shivering bones

Preparing me for what lies ahead

And I know she'll come again.

I know we will breathe spring again.

• • • 2020 • • •

Home isn't a place

It's a person

It's the feeling of opening my eyes each morning

And having you be the first thing I see

With the yellow sun glowing behind you

As we lay tangled in each other

Existing peacefully

It's the way your laughter is a song

That never ceases to make my heart do backflips

And fills me with an unyielding desire

To make you laugh and smile every day

It's the feeling of your hand in mine

As we take our leaps of faith

When all of a sudden, the air filling my lungs feels exciting

And I know there's nothing we can't do

I have found a home with you.

Translations and Notes

these are not official definitions but rather how I understand different terms

From *Dying*

Page 6

- Adhan: The voice calling muslims to prayer in mosques. Occurs 5 times a day at prayer times.
- Ramadan: Muslim holiday celebrating the deliverance of the Quran. A period of fasting

Page 8

- Zaghareet: a celebratory trilling sound
- Durbake: traditional Lebanese drum, goblet drum.
- 3amtous: 3amtou is the arabic word for paternal aunt, pluralized using American grammar to be "3amtous"

Page 21

- بسم الله الرحمن الرحيم: in the name of God, most merciful most kind
- Bismillah: "in the name of god"

From *Haunting*

- Halal: permissible or lawful in Islam
- Haram: Not permissible in Islam

From *Resurrecting*

- Eib: shameful or flawed

Acknowledgements

The thought of this book has existed in many forms since my family landed in the US in 2006, and I have many people to thank for how it has evolved and come into existence.

Most importantly, thank you to my husband Juwan Woods, for the emotional support and guidance given through this project, and showing me every day that happiness can exist in this world, and that those moments are worth writing about, too.

Thanks to my editor Monique Leblanc, I could not have done this without you and I hope you know that. You tirelessly supported me in a year where you certainly had other things to worry about, but you still made the time for me and without you this book would not have made it to the finish line.

To my wonderful pool of beta readers, Juanita Cox, Ashley Johnson, Maura Snell, and Katherine E. Soto. Thank you for your kind, encouraging eyes, and for the ways you made my poems stronger.

To my parents, thank you for being a model of strength and resilience that I have looked towards throughout life, for buying countless journals for me throughout my life, and stocking our shelves full of books since we were all kiddos. Passions don't come out of no where and this one for me has certainly come from the accessibility to art and knowledge you provided my whole life.

Thanks to some of the pivotal English teachers in my life, Laurie Pennington, Skip Fox, and Danielle Wheeler, for sparking a passion in me and helping maintain the fire. I have held on to the very specific words of encouragement each of you gave me through every creative adventure I have taken.

And finally, thanks to my cat Smoothie, for sitting on my lap during about 90% of this books creation, without your floof I wouldn't have felt the obligation of sitting perfectly still and motionless, which inevitably lead to me actually writing.

ABOUT THE AUTHOR

Nadia Rasha Khansa is a poet, artist, and trauma mental health thera-pist. This is her first published collection. In 2016 she gave the Tedx Talk "It's Time to Talk about Trauma" and has continued to empha-size the importance of art and self expression as necessary parts of healing in her work and personal life. She has previously been published as a freelance writer in Herstry Blog, Muftah Magazine, and she is a member of RAWI (The Radius of Arab American Writers).

instagram.com/vivohayati

goodreads.com/nadia_khansa

www.ingramcontent.com/pod-product-compliance
Lightning Source LLC
Chambersburg PA
CBHW071856020426
42331CB00010B/2545